THIS MANUAL IS MEANT TO BE USED.

Do not read it once and put it away.

Mark it up.

Run the protocols.

Circle what applies.

Cross out what does not.

Return to the work.

The Rural Revolution is not built by agreement.

It is built by action.

START WHERE YOU ARE.
USE WHAT YOU HAVE.
PUSH THE FLYWHEEL

· PINE CONE PRESS ·

THE RURAL REVOLUTION FIELD MANUAL

Volume One

Protocols for Rebuilding Small-Town Economies

C. Scott Stephens

PINE CONE PRESS

The Rural Revolution Field Manual
Volume One: Protocols for Rebuilding Small-Town Economies

Published by Pine Cone Press, an imprint of The Pine Cone Group LLC.

First Field Manual Edition
Printed in the United States of America.

Website: theruralrevolution.com

CONTENTS

THE RURAL ECONOMY FLYWHEEL

How the System Compounds

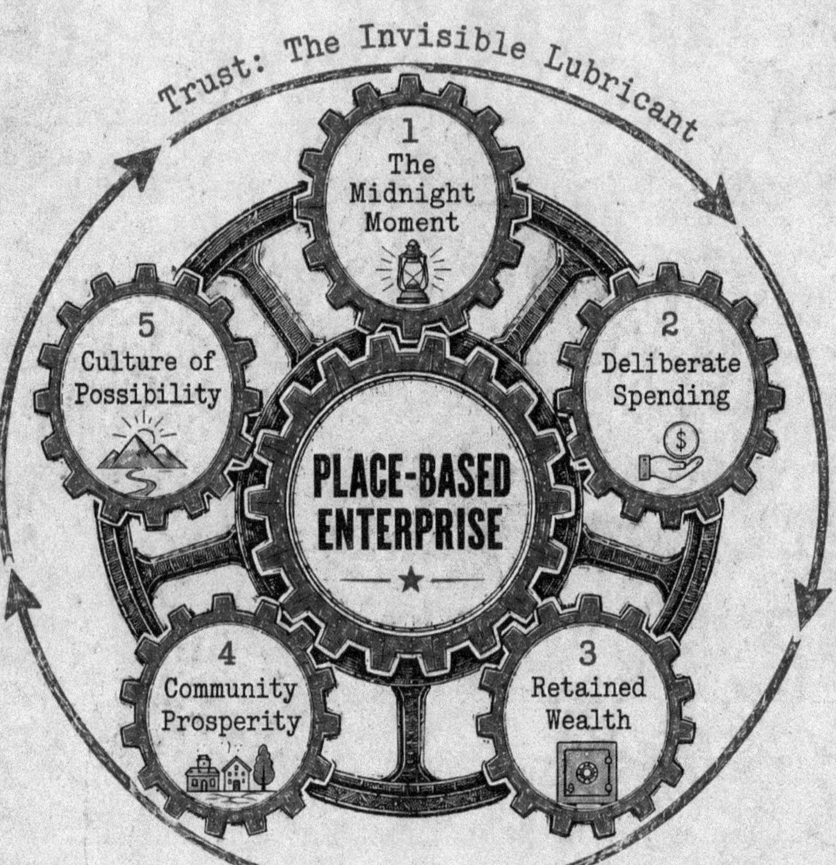

- **The Midnight Moment** — Someone decides to build.
- **Deliberate Spending** — Local dollars move with intention.
- **Retained Wealth** — Ownership keeps value close to home.
- **Community Prosperity** — Stability becomes visible.
- **Culture of Possibility** — Progress changes what people believe.

Each gear reinforces the next. Repeated action creates momentum.

HOW TO USE THIS BOOK

The Protocol System

This is not a book of ideas.
It is a system of execution.

Everything in The Rural Revolution is built around Protocols—clear, repeatable actions that move a place forward.

Why This Book Exists

This system was not built in theory.

It came from years of working directly with community organizations, local leaders, and small-town businesses—all asking the same question:

"How do we grow?"

They had:

- Good people
- Strong values
- A desire to improve
- But no clear starting point.
- No structure.
  No system.
  No shared language for action.

Meetings turned into conversations.
Conversations turned into ideas.
And ideas rarely turned into execution.

That gap is why this book exists.

The problem was never effort.
It was the absence of a repeatable way to act.

What Is a Protocol?

A Protocol is a specific action you can run.

Not theory.
Not inspiration.
Not "someday."

It is something you can do now, with what you already have.

Each Protocol is designed to:

- Remove guesswork
- Create consistency
- Produce visible results
- Run it once, you get movement.
  Run it repeatedly, you get momentum.

How the Numbering Works

Every Protocol follows a simple structure:

Protocol 3.1

3 = the system (the chapter)

- .1 = the action inside it

This turns the book into a working language:

- "We need to run 2.1."
- "That's a 7.1 gap."
- "Go back and rerun 1.1."
- When people start speaking this way, the system is working.

How the Protocols Work Together

Each chapter is a layer of the Flywheel.
Each Protocol is a turn of that wheel.

They are built to:

- Stand alone
- Stack together
- Compound over time
- This is not linear.
- You don't complete a Protocol—you return to it, sharper each time.
- That's how momentum builds.

The Standard

Before moving on, ask:

- "Did I run this?"
- Not:
- "Do I understand it?"
- "Do I agree with it?"
- But:
- "Did I apply it?"
- "Did it produce a result?"
- This system does not reward agreement.
  It rewards execution.

Where to Start

Start anywhere.

But don't stay theoretical.

Pick a Protocol.
Run it.
Observe what happens. Then run the next.

Final Note

- No permission is required.
- No perfect conditions are coming.
- The Flywheel only turns when someone decides to push.
- Run the first Protocol.

PROLOGUE: This is Not a Theory

The Proof of Concept: Denise and The Mossy Lantern

Most people look at a small-town Main Street and see a funeral in slow motion. They see empty storefronts, sun-bleached "For Lease" signs, and a quiet resignation that the digital age has finally won.

They're wrong.

In Atmore, Alabama, the air smells like old paper, fresh plaster, and "a little bit of magic". This is The Mossy Lantern, and it isn't just a bookstore. It's a middle finger to the idea that rural life has to be "less than."

The Calling vs. The Career

For Denise Respress, this wasn't a business plan—it was a calling that had been "quietly growing" like a spark that refused to be snuffed out. She didn't wait for a "someday" that might never come. She recognized that if a small town is going to survive, someone has to be brave enough to build the infrastructure for joy. "Atmore is home," she says. "It's where my roots are... and where community truly means something".

The Tactical Rescue

The Revolution doesn't require a bulldozer; it requires a vision. Denise executed a strategic takeover of a turn-key event space, formerly The Nelson Place, from fellow entrepreneur Tracey Nelson. She didn't just move in; she colonized the space with intentionality—adding the "magic" of hand-painted plaster and curated "cozy corners" that practically demand you slow down and breathe.

The "Chill Effect"

The shift was immediate. By creating a "Third Space" where people intentionally choose to linger, Denise didn't just build a business—she created a destination. Every person who walks through her door to find a story is a person who is now walking past three other local shops. She is the rising tide.

The Manifesto

Denise proves that in the New Rural Economy, your "why" is just as important as your "what". Her advice is the heartbeat of this book: "Go for it—but go in with heart, patience, and a willingness to be part of the community".

In a small town, you aren't just a merchant. You are a neighbor. If you show up consistently, support the person next to you, and create something genuine, the community won't just buy from you—they will fight for you.

Denise isn't just selling books. She's anchoring the heart of a revolution!

CHAPTER 1: THE ASSET TEST

Seeing What Actually Exists

You don't start by building.
You start by seeing.

Most people skip this. They jump straight to ideas, funding, or plans without understanding the ground they're standing on. That's why most efforts stall. They're built on assumptions instead of assets.

There are roughly 19,500 incorporated places in the United States. If you define a small town as under 5,000 people, about 76% of them qualify. That's 14,000 to 15,000 towns. Nearly half of those have fewer than 500 people.

So no—your situation isn't unique. The constraints aren't unique. The opportunity isn't either.

Most towns don't fail because they lack assets. They fail because they misidentify what assets are. People look for outside capital, large employers, or perfect conditions. When those aren't present, they default to the same conclusion: there's nothing here.

That's not an economic reality. It's a perception failure.

The Asset Test Framework

Before anything is built, every town must be evaluated across three categories: Practical Assets, Social Assets, and Stability Assets.

Each one answers a different question. Where can I start? Who will carry it? What is worth keeping?

PROTOCOL 1.1: PRACTICAL ASSET AUDIT

What can be used right now

Do not start with ideas. Start with inventory.

Begin with what is already sitting idle. Vacant storefronts, underutilized buildings, unused land, equipment that hasn't been touched in years. These are not signs of decline. They are pre-built opportunities.

An empty building isn't just a reminder of what failed. It's a structure that already exists—walls, wiring, location—all in place. In most small towns, the cost to occupy that space is a fraction of what it would be in a city. That matters.

Next, measure friction. How long does it actually take to open a business? Who approves it? How many steps are involved? In rural communities, the process is often simpler than people assume—but no one has taken the time to define it clearly.

Then test flexibility. Talk to property owners. Talk to local officials. Talk to existing business owners. You are looking for one thing: is there room to try?

If the answer is yes, you have something most cities don't—low-cost experimentation.

By the end of this protocol, you should be able to name three to five spaces you could operate in, understand the real cost to enter, and clearly define the actual barriers. Not assumed ones. Real ones.

If you can't do that, you're not ready to build.

PROTOCOL 1.2: TRUST NETWORK MAPPING

Who actually moves information

In small towns, marketing is not the driver. Trust is.

In a city, attention is expensive. In a small town, attention is already there. What matters is reputation. People are watching, talking, and remembering. A recommendation from the right person carries more weight than any ad campaign. A bad experience travels even faster.

Every town has a trust network. The question is whether you know where it lives.

Start by identifying connectors. These are the people who seem to know everyone, hear everything, and influence decisions without holding formal positions. Every town has them.

Then identify where people gather. Coffee shops, churches, feed stores, local businesses. These aren't just places. They're distribution channels for information.

Pay attention to how people talk. Who gets recommended? Who gets warned about? What stories keep coming up? That tells you what the market actually values.

And then, enter the network the right way. You don't hack trust. You earn it. You show up consistently. You do what you say you're going to do. You treat people right when it's not convenient.

Over time, something shifts. The community doesn't just notice your business—they start to carry it. They talk about it. They protect it. They bring others to it.

By the end of this protocol, you should know who the key connectors are, where influence concentrates, and how reputation actually moves through your town. If you don't know that, you're operating blind.

PROTOCOL 1.3: STABILITY ASSET IDENTIFICATION

What is built to last

This is the layer most people ignore because it doesn't produce quick wins. But it determines whether anything you build actually sticks.

Start by identifying long-term businesses. The ones that have been around for decades. The ones people trust without thinking about it. These aren't just businesses—they're anchors. They hold relationships, history, and continuity.

Then assess ownership risk. Who owns these businesses? Are they nearing exit? Is there a plan for what happens next? If there isn't, that asset is at risk of disappearing.

Next, evaluate transfer potential. Can the business be purchased, partnered with, or transitioned? Sometimes the best move isn't starting something new. It's stepping into something that already works and keeping it alive.

Finally, define the time horizon. Every decision has to answer a simple question: is this built for two years, or twenty?

If it's not built to last, it won't strengthen the town.

By the end of this protocol, you should be able to identify several businesses worth protecting, possible transition opportunities, and where ownership gaps exist.

Putting It Together

When you run all three protocols, something changes. The town stops looking like a place that's behind and starts looking like a place that's ready.

You know where you can operate. You know who will influence your success. You know what actually matters long-term.

Most people are waiting on capital, permission, or timing. None of those come first. Clarity does.

Chapter Close

You are not starting from zero.

You are starting with existing structures, existing relationships, and existing systems. The problem was never absence. It was visibility.

The work begins here.

Not with building.

With seeing.

Because once you can see clearly, you don't need permission. You don't need perfect conditions. You just need to start.

CHAPTER 2: THE MIDNIGHT MOMENT

The Drive Gear

On a stretch of downtown in Atmore, Alabama, a storefront operates that would not exist if someone had waited for better conditions. Inside The Mossy Lantern, the shelves are filled with books, gifts, and locally relevant goods. The space is not large, and it was not built on outside investment or population growth.

It exists because someone chose to act.

Denise Respress identified a gap in her community and moved on it. That decision created more than a business. It introduced a new point of activity into the local economy and demonstrated that investment was still viable in that location.

This is the Midnight Moment.

It is the point where an individual moves from observation to action. Without it, no system forms. With it, activity begins.

A town's economic direction is not determined by population alone. It is determined by the number of individuals actively building within it. Communities of similar size can produce different outcomes depending on how many people move into ownership and operation.

The constraint is not awareness.

Most communities have individuals who recognize gaps. They discuss ideas, identify needs, and in some cases begin informal work. These efforts rarely convert into operating businesses.

The reason is structural.

Ideas remain informal because there is no process to move them into defined action. Without definition, they do not enter the market. Without market entry, there is no visible change. Without visible change, no additional participation follows.

Over time, this creates a false read of the environment. The conclusion becomes that there are no builders. In practice, there are individuals close to action who have not been moved forward.

- The requirement is not to find new people.
- It is to convert existing people into operators.

That conversion does not happen passively. It requires intervention from organizations that already have access to these individuals—business groups, economic development organizations, and established operators within the community.

Their role is not to promote activity.

It is to structure it.

Protocol 2.1: Dreamer Seminar

The first step is to move individuals from informal thinking into defined action.

This is done through a controlled working session. The purpose is not networking or instruction. It is to take undeveloped ideas and force clarity.

Participants are selected based on proximity to action. These are individuals who have already demonstrated interest through side work, repeated discussion, or partial execution. They are not beginners, and they are not observers.

The session is led by operators who have built businesses. Their role is to remove unnecessary complexity and define a starting point.

Each participant leaves with a clear statement of what they are building, how it produces revenue, and what the first step is within a defined time frame.

- The output is not a finished business.
- It is a defined entry point.

This step addresses the primary failure point at the idea stage. It converts informal thinking into structured intent.

It also introduces visibility between participants. Individuals observe others moving forward, which reduces perceived risk and increases the likelihood of follow-through.

Protocol 2.2: Shared-Risk Incubation

Once an individual decides to act, the next constraint is initial cost and commitment.

Rent, utilities, and long-term agreements create a barrier that exceeds the level of certainty most early-stage operators have. This prevents conversion from intent to execution.

The solution is to reduce concentrated risk.

This is accomplished through shared operating environments. Instead of requiring a single operator to take on a full space, multiple early-stage operators occupy the same location and divide cost.

This model is in use in places such as Ozark AL through the Ozark-Dale County Economic Development Corporation incubator. The primary impact is behavioral.

Lower cost reduces hesitation. Shared space reduces isolation. Activity becomes visible within the environment.

Operators observe each other working. Information moves informally. Mistakes are corrected faster. Early-stage progress becomes repeatable across participants.

This reduces the time required to reach functional operation.

The incubator is not optimized for presentation.

- It is optimized for throughput.

Its role is to allow multiple businesses to begin at the same time under conditions that make early execution possible.

Protocol 2.3: Diversification Loop

Individual action does not create system change.

Repeated action does. When a business begins operation, it activates space and introduces visible activity. This alters perception of the immediate environment.

Additional individuals observe this change and reassess the feasibility of their own entry. Some convert to action. This creates a sequence.

A business opens. Activity becomes visible. Another individual acts. Additional businesses form. This repetition produces a distributed base of operators. The outcome is a local economy that is not dependent on a single employer or sector. Instead, it is supported by multiple independent operations.

This structure is more stable. Failures at the individual level do not collapse the system because activity is distributed. This is the mechanism by which resilience forms.

What Organizations Are Responsible For

Organizations already have access to individuals within the community. They control environments where people gather and exchange information.

The shift is functional.

Instead of maintaining passive environments, they create conditions where action is defined and initiated.

This includes:

- Identifying individuals close to action
- Forcing clarity at the idea stage
- Reducing initial operating risk
- Allowing multiple operators to begin simultaneously
- The objective is not to produce a single successful business.
- It is to increase the number of individuals entering operation.

As participation increases, activity becomes visible. As activity becomes visible, additional participation follows.

The system reinforces itself.

Chapter Close

The Midnight Moment is the starting point of the system.

It introduces motion.

However, motion alone does not sustain activity.

The continuation of the system depends on how revenue circulates once businesses are operating.

That is the next stage.

Deliberate Spending. The Fuel.

CHAPTER 3: THE RURAL COMPETITIVE ADVANTAGE

High-Trust, Low-Cap Operations

Before a flywheel can spin, it must overcome resistance.

In cities, resistance is constant. High rent compresses time. Competition forces reaction. Scale is required before stability. Capital is concentrated, but so is friction. Every decision carries weight. Every mistake carries cost. Survival depends on speed.

Rural markets operate differently.

They reduce friction where ideas are most fragile. Lower cost. Longer runway. More time to stabilize before pressure forces failure. This creates something cities cannot offer.

Leverage.

This is the Rural Competitive Advantage.

Not competing with cities.
Building where the rules are different.

This advantage sits at the beginning of the flywheel—inside The Midnight Moment. It allows an idea to move from thought to operation without being crushed by overhead.

Chapter 1 created visibility.
Chapter 2 created structure.
Chapter 3 creates action.

Protocol 3.1: Build the Rural Moat

You are not operating in a smaller version of a city.

You are operating inside a different system.

Your job is not to imitate urban models. Your job is to use rural conditions as leverage. These conditions form your moat—the built-in protection that allows a business to survive early, stabilize, and expand.

Four commands activate it.

Command 1: Convert Low Overhead Into Time

(Flywheel Link: The Midnight Moment ⊠ The Drive Gear)

Lower costs extend time. Time increases survivability.

Use reduced rent, labor, and operating expenses to lengthen your runway. Delay pressure. Test, adjust, and refine before scaling.

In cities, time is expensive.
In rural markets, time can be created.

- Do not trade it for speed.
- Use it to build something that holds.

Command 2: Expand Your Market Radius

(Flywheel Link: Deliberate Spending ⊠ The Fuel)

- You are not serving foot traffic. You are capturing radius.
- In a rural economy, customers will travel for value, quality, and experience. Your market is not a block. It is a region.
- Stop thinking like a storefront. Think in driving distance.

When you do this, you are no longer competing locally. You are capturing intentional spending across your trade area. That is how leakage is reduced and local circulation begins.

Command 3: Compound Relationship Equity

(Flywheel Link: Retained Wealth ⊠ The Lock)

- Trust is the operating currency of rural markets.
- Every interaction builds or erodes it. Names matter. Consistency matters. Problem-solving matters. Accessibility matters.
- Reduce friction by being known and reliable. Solve problems quickly. Show up repeatedly.
- Trust compounds faster than capital.
- Over time, it becomes a protective layer competitors cannot

penetrate. This is how money stays local—not just through ownership, but through behavior.

Field Report — Hardware Store

For six years, Paul Smith and his wife lived in a basement on forty dollars a week, holding a hardware store together. Not growing. Not expanding. Keeping it alive.

He didn't come into it blind. He grew up around construction—his grandfather and father were builders. The assumption was he would follow that path. Instead, a job in a local grocery store shifted it. He saw what a long-standing local business actually was. Not just transactions. Continuity. Relationships. Stability inside a town.

At twenty-three, he bought a hardware store.

What followed was pressure.

Thin margins.
Limited cash.
Years where quitting would have been the logical move.

In a rural town, that is where most businesses fail.

Because the numbers alone rarely justify staying.

The store solved problems people could not delay—broken gates, water lines, roof leaks, jobs that had to keep moving. Leaving town cost time. Waiting cost progress. So people came local, not always for price, but for access, speed, and certainty.

Over time, that behavior stabilized the business.

Not marketing.
Not scale.

Repetition.

The flood exposed what the business actually was.

Water rose from the creek behind the property. Inventory at risk. Building going under. There was no plan for it.

The town responded anyway.

Forklifts arrived from other businesses. Inventory moved. A nearby warehouse opened. People showed up without being asked.

No coordination.
No delay.

By the next morning, the store reopened.

Operational.

That is not customer loyalty.

That is a system recognizing something it depends on.

What kept him there wasn't just obligation. It was recognition.

He had seen what a multi-generation business meant to a community. He understood that if the store survived, something larger survived with it. If it failed, something would be lost that would not easily be replaced.

That shifted the decision.

It was no longer about income. It was about function.

There were opportunities to leave.

More money.
More stability.
Cleaner paths.

That option looks rational.

It isn't.

Because when an anchor leaves, the loss spreads. Work slows. Decisions shift outward. Dependence increases. The system weakens in ways that are not immediately visible, but are difficult to reverse.

Paul stayed.

He ran that business for fourteen years.

Then he transitioned out of it—not into something easier, but into something larger.

Today, he is the Senior Pastor of Rivertown Community Church, rivertown. cc, a multi-site church operating across multiple rural communities.

Same pattern. Different system.

Building trust.
Creating structure.
Stabilizing people.
Holding a network together.

Amen.

The skillset transferred because the function was the same.

Lead people.
Solve real problems.
Stay consistent.
Earn trust over time.

That is not a career shift.

That is system continuity.

Protocol 3.2 — The Anchor Principle

A hardware store is a repair system. Remove it, and the town loses response time. Remove enough of these, and the town loses function.

Anchor businesses are structural.

Protocol 3.3 — The Confidence Loop

Local spending keeps money in circulation. Circulation stabilizes businesses. Stability builds trust. Trust reinforces local spending.

That loop is the economy.

Break it, and decline compounds.

Command 4: Leverage Visible Momentum

(Flywheel Link: Community Prosperity ⊠ The Output)

In a small town, progress is never invisible.

A new business is noticed. A restored building is discussed. A risk taken is felt across the community. This visibility is not pressure—it is propulsion.

Use it.

Every action you take sends a signal. Every improvement creates belief. And belief is what turns individual effort into collective momentum.

You are not operating in isolation.

You are contributing to the visible output of the flywheel.

The Rural Competitive Advantage is not about having more.

It is about using what you have with precision.

Lower costs become longer runways.
Smaller populations become stronger networks.
Slower pace becomes a strategic filter.

When these commands are executed together, something powerful happens.

The barrier to entry lowers.
The risk of failure decreases.
And the probability of survival—and eventual dominance—rises.

That is how the flywheel begins to turn.

Not with scale. But with leverage applied in the right place, at the right time, under the right conditions.

CHAPTER 4: PLACE AS STRATEGY

Rooting the Business Model

The Thesis:
Location is not a limitation. It is leverage. In rural America, geography is not a backdrop to your business—it is the business.

Most people misunderstand this. They see a small town and think in terms of what is missing—traffic, density, capital, convenience. They attempt to import a model that was designed for somewhere else and then wonder why it struggles to take root.

But the advantage is not in imitation. The advantage is in alignment.

A rural business that works is one that cannot be lifted out of its soil without losing its identity. It belongs to the place. It draws from it. It reinforces it. And in doing so, it becomes defensible in a way no chain ever can be.

This is how Place becomes Strategy.

And when done correctly, it becomes one of the strongest accelerants in the Rural Economy Flywheel.

Because a business rooted in place does more than generate revenue—it deepens Deliberate Spending (The Fuel), strengthens Retained Wealth (The Lockbox), and visibly contributes to Community Prosperity (The Output).

Protocol 4.1: The Authenticity Filter

If it could exist anywhere, it would eventually be replaced.

The goal is not to build a "good business." The goal is to build a business that only makes sense here.

The Authenticity Filter is how you test that.

1. Asset Alignment

Every town already has raw material. Most just don't recognize it as such.

If the land is agricultural, the business should reflect the land.
If the town sits on a river, the river should show up in the experience.
If the architecture tells a story, the business should continue that story.

This is not branding. This is integration.

A restaurant that sources locally is not just buying ingredients—it is embedding itself into the regional economy. A retail store that reflects the working culture of the community is not just selling goods—it is signaling belonging.

This alignment feeds the Flywheel directly:

- It gives locals a reason to choose you (Deliberate Spending)
- It keeps suppliers circulating nearby (Retained Wealth)
- It creates a business that people are proud to point to (Community Prosperity)
- When the business reflects the place, the place begins to defend the business.

2. Gap Identification (Market Leakage)

Every rural town has a quiet habit: it exports its money.

Not intentionally. Not maliciously. But consistently.

People drive 20, 30, sometimes 50 miles to solve problems that could be solved locally. Hardware. Clothing. Coffee. Services. Experiences.

This is "Market Leakage."

And it is one of the clearest signals you will ever get.

Instead of asking, "What business should I start?"
Ask, "What are we already paying for somewhere else?"

That answer is your blueprint.

Because unlike guessing at demand, this is proven demand. The customer already exists. The behavior is already established. The only thing missing is proximity.

When you plug a leak:

- You captured spending that was leaving (Deliberate Spending)
- You keep that capital cycling locally (Retained Wealth)
- You reduce dependency on outside systems (Community Prosperity)
- This is not speculation. This is redirection.

3. *Strategic Storytelling*

Every small town has something most modern businesses cannot manufacture continuity.

History. Buildings. Families. Stories. Memory.

These are not sentimental assets—they are economic ones.

A business that intentionally ties itself to these elements becomes more than a transaction point. It becomes a signal.

A signal that says: this place matters.

A restored building on Main Street is not just a renovation. It is proof of belief. It tells the next builder that something is happening here. It creates what we call the Signal Effect—visible momentum that invites participation.

This is where Place Strategy compounds.

Because storytelling does three things simultaneously:

- It increases emotional attachment (driving Deliberate Spending)
- It builds long-term identity (supporting Retained Wealth)
- It creates visible progress (fueling Community Prosperity)

And over time, it contributes to something even more important:

A Culture of Possibility.

Where people stop asking, "Why would you do that here?"
And start asking, "What could we build next?"

The Flywheel Connection

Place is not a separate idea from the Flywheel—it is the terrain it spins on.

A business that ignores its geography creates friction.
A business that aligns with its geography creates momentum.

It lowers risk because it serves known demand

It increases loyalty because it reflects shared identity

It strengthens the local economy because it keeps value embedded

And most importantly, it becomes harder to replace.

Because a chain can replicate a product.
It cannot replicate a place.

Closing

The goal is not to escape where you are.

The goal is to see it clearly enough to use it.

Your town is not behind.
It is underutilized.

And once you begin to treat Place as Strategy, you stop building businesses that survive despite where they are...

...and start building ones that thrive because of it.

CHAPTER 5: TRUST AS INFRASTRUCTURE

Building and Social Capital

The Thesis: Trust is not a feeling; it is infrastructure. In rural markets, it functions as the "invisible broadband" that reduces friction, lowers cost, and accelerates economic activity.

Trust is the system beneath the system. While cities rely on process, contracts, and scale to move commerce forward, rural economies rely on reputation. That is not a limitation, it is an advantage. When trust is high, transactions happen faster, partnerships form easier, and businesses operate with less drag.

A handshake carries weight because it is backed by history. A name carries leverage because it has been tested over time. In this environment, credibility becomes currency, and consistency becomes compounding capital.

This is where rural markets outperform. Trust replaces layers of verification. It shortens the distance between introduction and transaction. It turns relationships into operating infrastructure.

(Flywheel Impact: Trust reduces friction across all four gears—accelerating The Midnight Moment, reinforcing Deliberate Spending, protecting Retained Wealth, and stabilizing Community Prosperity.)

Protocol 5.1: The Accountability Loop

Reputation is the enforcement mechanism of the rural economy.

In a small town, word-of-mouth is not marketing—it is infrastructure. Your reputation enters the room before you do and remains after you leave. Every interaction either strengthens or weakens the system you depend on.

- Stand Behind the Work: Fix mistakes quickly and visibly. Accountability builds more trust than perfection.
- Protect the Name: Margin can recover. Reputation rarely does.
- Consistency Over Time: Trust compounds through repeated proof,

not one-time performance.

A business that answers for itself becomes reliable. A reliable business becomes preferred. A preferred business becomes protected.

(Flywheel Tie-In: A strong Accountability Loop builds the confidence required for others to step into The Midnight Moment and fuels Deliberate Spending through trust-based purchasing.)

Protocol 5.2: The Network Effect

Economic strength is built through relationships, not isolation.

No rural business operates alone. The strongest markets function as interconnected ecosystems of informal partnership suppliers, service providers, tradesmen, and owners working in alignment.

- Handshake Agreements: Trust reduces the need for friction-heavy contracts.
- Local Supply Chains: Keep transactions inside the community whenever possible.
- Mutual Reinforcement: One business growing should create lift for others.

This is not charity, it is strategy. A connected economy circulates dollars more efficiently and withstands disruption more effectively.

(Flywheel Tie-In: The Network Effect strengthens Retained Wealth by keeping dollars local and accelerating Community Prosperity through cooperative growth.)

Protocol 5.3: Trust Acquisition

Invest time before capital.

For new entrepreneurs, trust is not assumed—it is earned. Entering a rural market without social capital creates friction that no amount of funding can overcome.

- Earn the Goodwill License: Participate in civic life before expecting economic return.
- Show Up Consistently: Meetings, events, conversations—presence builds familiarity.
- Respect Place: Learn history before attempting to reshape it.

The community must believe you are rooted, not extracting. Once that belief is established, opportunity begins to move toward you rather than away from you.

(Flywheel Tie-In: Trust Acquisition lowers the barrier to The Midnight Moment and ensures long-term alignment with Community Prosperity.)

The Outcome: Trust as Scale

In rural economies, trust is scale.

It is how small towns achieve efficiency without bureaucracy. It is how businesses grow without massive overhead. It is how communities remain resilient without centralized control.

A trusted business gains more than customers, it gains advocates, partners, and patience. It becomes embedded in the local system, making it harder to replace and easier to sustain.

When trust is strong, the economy moves with less resistance. When it is weak, everything slows down.

Trust is not extra. It is the infrastructure that makes everything else work.

(Final Flywheel Integration: Trust is the lubricant of the entire system—allowing all four gears to spin faster, smoother, and longer while reinforcing a Culture of Possibility across the community.)

CHAPTER 6: BUSINESSES DESIGNED TO STAY

The Longevity Over Scale Framework

The Thesis

In modern business culture, success is often measured by speed—how fast you can grow, how quickly you can scale, and ultimately, how soon you can exit. Venture-backed models celebrate the flip. Build it, grow it, sell it. Move on.

But in rural America, this model does more harm than good.

Because when a business exits, it doesn't just change ownership—it often breaks trust, drains wealth, and weakens the very foundation that allowed it to succeed in the first place.

A rural business is not just a revenue engine. It is part of the town's operating system.

The goal, then, is not scale for the sake of scale. The goal is permanence.

A true Community Anchor is not built to exit. It is built to endure.

It is designed to still be standing in twenty years, still serving the same families, still circulating money locally, and still reinforcing the identity of the place it calls home. This is where the Rural Economy Flywheel gains real torque—not from rapid acceleration, but from sustained, intentional motion over time.

(Retained Wealth ☒ Community Prosperity ☒ Culture of Possibility)

Protocol 6.1: The Continuity Audit

The first shift an entrepreneur must make is redefining the time horizon.

Most businesses make decisions based on quarterly results or annual growth targets. A Community Anchor makes decisions based on decades.

This is the Continuity Audit—a simple but powerful filter applied to every major decision:

- "Will this action help ensure we are still here in twenty years?"
- This question changes everything.

It changes how you hire.
It changes how you price.
It changes how you expand.
It changes what opportunities you say no to.

Because not every profitable move is a durable one.

A cheap supplier might improve margins today but erode quality tomorrow. A rapid expansion might increase revenue but stretch operations beyond what the community can support. A private equity buyout might offer a large payday but remove the business from local control entirely.

The Continuity Audit forces discipline. It demands that short-term gains be weighed against long-term presence.

In this framework, growth is not eliminated—it is refined. It becomes slower, steadier, and far more resilient.

This is how businesses transition from being temporary participants in a market to permanent fixtures in a community.

And permanence is where real economic power begins to accumulate.

(Retained Wealth: decisions that keep ownership, profit, and control local over time.)

Protocol 6.2: Generational Loyalty

A business that lasts twenty years does not survive on transactions alone. It survives on relationships that compound.

This is the concept of Generational Loyalty.

In a rural town, the most valuable customer is not the one who spends the most today. It is the family that keeps coming back—year after year, decade after decade.

The father who bought his tools there.

The daughter who now brings her own children.
The grandson who doesn't even consider going anywhere else.

This is not brand loyalty in the modern marketing sense. This is inheritance.

And it cannot be replicated by a national chain.

Chains compete on convenience and price. Community Anchors compete on memory, trust, and identity.

To build Generational Loyalty, a business must intentionally design for it.

That means consistency in product and service.
It means faces that customers recognize over time.
It means stories that are tied to the place itself.

It also means resisting the temptation to constantly reinvent in pursuit of trends. Stability is not stagnation—it is signal. It tells the community that this place can be counted on.

Over time, that signal becomes an asset.

A Permanence Asset.

One that lowers customer acquisition costs to near zero, increases lifetime value beyond any modern metric, and reinforces the social fabric of the town itself.

This is where the Flywheel accelerates again.

Because when loyalty spans generations, spending becomes deliberate, local, and habitual.

(Deliberate Spending ⊠ Retained Wealth)

Protocol 6.3: The Employment Anchor

A business does not become a Community Anchor on revenue alone. It becomes one through people.

Specifically, through stable, local employment.

(Community Prosperity: visible stability, stronger households, and a more resilient local economy.)

The Long View

The Longevity Over Scale Framework is not anti-growth. It is anti-fragility.

It rejects the idea that success must be fast, extractive, and temporary. Instead, it embraces a model where success is measured in years of presence, depth of relationships, and consistency of impact.

A business designed to stay does not chase every opportunity. It selects the right ones.

It does not expand beyond its ability to serve well.
It does not dilute its identity to appeal to everyone.
It does not sacrifice trust for short-term gain.

Instead, it compounds.

Slowly. Intentionally. Powerfully.

And over time, that compounding creates something far more valuable than a quick exit ever could.

It creates a cornerstone.

A place people rely on.
A place people recognize.
A place people fight to keep.

This is the final shift in mindset for the rural entrepreneur.

You are not just building a business.

You are building something that should outlast you.

In many growth-focused models, labor is treated as a variable cost—something to optimize, reduce, or replace. But in a rural economy, jobs are not just expenses. They are economic infrastructure.

Every stable job supports a household.
Every household supports other local businesses.
Every paycheck circulates through the community multiple times.

This is the Local Multiplier Effect in action.

When a business prioritizes consistent employment over aggressive expansion, it creates a stabilizing force within the town. Employees stay longer. Skills deepen. Trust builds internally just as it does externally.

Contrast this with high-turnover models or businesses designed for quick scaling and exit. Jobs become temporary. Knowledge leaves. The economic impact becomes shallow and short-lived.

The Employment Anchor flips this entirely.

It asks:
How do we create roles that people can grow into—not just pass through?
How do we build a team that sees this business as part of their life, not just a stop along the way?

Because when employees are rooted, the business becomes rooted.

And when the business is rooted, the community gains strength.

The Flywheel Connection

When businesses are designed to stay, the entire Rural Economy Flywheel stabilizes and strengthens.

The Midnight Moment sparks new builders—but now they see a path that lasts.

Deliberate Spending increases because trust and loyalty deepen.

Retained Wealth compounds as ownership remains local across decades.

Community Prosperity becomes visible through stable jobs and enduring institutions.

And ultimately, a Culture of Possibility takes hold—because people can see, with their own eyes, that building something lasting is not only possible, it is already happening.

This is how a town stops cycling through fragile ideas and starts building permanent momentum.

Not through scale.

But through staying.

CHAPTER 7: STORY AS ECONOMIC SIGNAL

Narrative Management for Growth

The Thesis:
A town's economic trajectory is not set by population charts or outside investment—it is shaped by the stories its people repeat, reinforce, and broadcast. Markets, investors, and even future residents respond to perception before data. If the dominant narrative is decline, capital stays away. If the dominant narrative is momentum, capital leans in.

Story is not decoration.
Story is signal.

Perception is Reality

Every renovated storefront, every new business license, every risk taken by a local entrepreneur sends a message to the outside world: something is happening here. The question is whether that message is amplified—or lost.

The work, then, is intentional. You must actively replace the inherited Narrative of Decline with a consistent, visible Signal of Possibility.

This is not about spin. It is about alignment—ensuring that real progress is seen, repeated, and believed.

(Flywheel Tie-In: Culture of Possibility — Story is the carrier wave that sustains belief and attracts new energy into the system.)

Protocol 7.1: The Visibility Strategy

Turning Local Progress into Market Signals

Most small towns make a critical mistake: they do the work, but they do not tell the story.

A building gets renovated quietly.
A new business opens with little fanfare.
An entrepreneur takes a risk—and only a handful of people notice.

In a rural economy, this is a missed opportunity of the highest order.

Every act of progress must be treated as a public signal.

The Visibility Strategy is simple in concept but powerful in execution: You intentionally document and distribute proof that the town is moving forward.

This includes:

- Featuring every new business, expansion, or renovation
- Highlighting local entrepreneurs as builders, not just owners
- Creating consistent media touchpoints (newsletters, magazines, social channels)
- Repeating wins until they become identity

A platform like The River Ledger is not just a newsletter—it is economic infrastructure. It functions as a real-time ticker of local momentum. Each story becomes a signal to three audiences simultaneously:

- Residents — reinforcing pride and participation
- Entrepreneurs — lowering perceived risk to start something new
- Outsiders — signaling that the town is investable

When done correctly, visibility compounds. One story leads to another. One opening leads to two more. Momentum becomes self-reinforcing.

(Flywheel Tie-In: The Midnight Moment — Stories of others taking action reduce hesitation and spark new builders.)
(Flywheel Tie-In: Deliberate Spending — Visibility directs dollars toward local businesses.)

Protocol 7.2: Identity Branding

Building "Authenticity Equity" Through Place

In rural markets, brand is not separate from place—it is derived from it.

The strongest businesses do not try to look like everywhere else.
They become unmistakably tied to where they are.

This is where Authenticity Equity is built.

A business rooted in its geography—its land, its history, its people—cannot be easily replicated by a national chain. It carries narrative weight that outsiders cannot manufacture.

Identity Branding requires intentional decisions:

- Incorporating local materials, stories, or traditions into products and services
- Referencing regional history in naming, design, and experience
- Reflecting the landscape in the business model itself

Positioning the business as a continuation of the town's story—not a replacement of it

This does two things simultaneously:

- It deepens loyalty within the community
- It differentiates the business externally
- A visitor should immediately understand: this could only exist here.

That uniqueness becomes economic leverage. It attracts tourism, attention, and dollars that would never flow to something generic.

(Flywheel Tie-In: Retained Wealth — Authentic businesses are harder to replace, keeping dollars local.)

Protocol 7.3: Replication Without Extraction

Scaling the Signal, Not Selling the Core

Here is where many communities get it wrong.

They confuse growth with exit.
They believe the only way to scale is to sell, franchise, or dilute what made the business valuable in the first place.

But there is another path.

You can replicate the system without surrendering the ownership.

A strong rural business should think in terms of repeatable models, not just single locations:

- Documented processes and playbooks
- Brand standards rooted in place
- Operational systems that can be taught and transferred
- Media and storytelling frameworks that travel with the model
- This allows for expansion in ways that extend the story rather than erase it.
- For example:
- A concept can expand regionally while maintaining local ownership in each location
- A product line can scale digitally while still being produced locally
- A brand can grow its audience nationally while keeping its physical roots intact
- The key principle is this:
  Scale the narrative, not the extraction.

If growth removes ownership from the community, it breaks the flywheel.
If growth amplifies local ownership, it accelerates it.

(Flywheel Tie-In: Community Prosperity — Growth that maintains local ownership increases shared outcomes.)

The Outcome: A Self-Reinforcing Signal

When story is managed correctly, the town begins to change in a measurable way.

Perception shifts first.
Then behavior follows.
Then economics respond.

Residents begin to believe in the future again.
Entrepreneurs see opportunity instead of risk.
Investors recognize momentum instead of decline.

And perhaps most importantly—the next generation sees a place worth staying for.

This is how a small town moves from quiet survival to visible growth.

Not through a single project.
Not through outside rescue.

But through a consistent, amplified signal.

CHAPTER 8: THE MAIN STREET ENTREPRENEUR

Protocol: From Operator to Capital Magnet

The rural economy does not fail because of a lack of ideas. It fails because of a lack of operators willing to act on obvious needs. Before capital flows, before outside attention arrives, before systems are built, there must be someone willing to open the door, turn on the lights, and serve the first customer.

This is the role of the Main Street Entrepreneur.

They are not venture-backed. They are not chasing scale. They are not optimizing for exit. They are solving for usefulness. The Main Street Entrepreneur is the individual who looks at a daily inconvenience in their town and decides to remove it. A missing service. A closed storefront. A gap everyone complains about but no one claims. Where others see decline, they see a job to be done.

This is the activation point of the flywheel—the human trigger that turns The Midnight Moment into something visible. Because once a business opens, the theory of possibility becomes proof. People no longer have to imagine what could happen. They can see it.

And when people can see it, behavior begins to change.

Money that once leaked out of town begins to slow down. A family that used to drive thirty minutes for a service now spends locally. A contractor finds a nearby supplier instead of ordering from outside the region. A visitor has a reason to stop instead of pass through. This is the early stage of Deliberate Spending—not as a campaign, but as a byproduct of usefulness.

But here is where most communities misunderstand what is happening.

They assume the entrepreneur is the outcome.

In reality, the entrepreneur is the signal.

A single business does not transform a town. But it does something far more important: it proves that transformation is possible. It sends a message to three critical audiences at once:

- To residents: "You don't have to leave to build something."
- To other potential operators: "There is still room here."

To capital: "This place is active, not abandoned."

This is where the role of the Main Street Entrepreneur shifts from operator to indicator. The business itself matters—but the signal it sends matters more.

Because capital does not move first. It follows movement.

Banks, lenders, landlords, and even informal investors are not in the business of taking blind risk. They are in the business of recognizing patterns. And the clearest pattern they look for is simple: Is anything working here?

The Main Street Entrepreneur answers that question.

A full parking lot on a Friday night answers that question.
A booked-out service calendar answers that question.
A steady line at a counter answers that question.

These are not just signs of a healthy business. They are signals to capital that the town has demand worth serving.

This is why the first entrepreneur in a struggling market is disproportionately important. They are not just building revenue for themselves. They are lowering perceived risk for everyone who comes after them.

In flywheel terms, this is where Deliberate Spending begins to convert into Retained Wealth. Because once money starts circulating locally with consistency, it creates something that can be measured, underwritten, and ultimately financed.

But this transition does not happen automatically.

Most rural communities stop at encouragement. They celebrate the new business, post about it on social media, maybe even host a ribbon cutting—and then assume the job is done. What they fail to do is capture the signal and translate it into structured opportunity.

That requires a shift in thinking.

Instead of asking, "How do we support this one business?" the better question becomes:
"How do we use this business as proof to unlock the next five?"

This is where the concept of the tent people becomes critical.

The next wave of entrepreneurs is rarely sitting in a boardroom waiting to be discovered. They are already operating at the edge of the market—selling at festivals, testing products at markets, running side businesses out of garages, food trucks, trailers, and temporary setups. They are watching closely. Not just for encouragement, but for evidence.

They are asking:
"Will this town actually support something new?"
"Is it worth the risk to go all in?"

When they see a Main Street business succeed—not just open, but sustain—they get their answer.

This is how one entrepreneur becomes two.
Two becomes five.
Five becomes a pattern.

And patterns are what capital understands.

At this stage, the role of leadership—formal or informal—must evolve. It is no longer enough to cheer from the sidelines. The community must begin lowering friction for the next operators:

- Making small storefronts accessible instead of sitting vacant
- Encouraging flexible leases for first-time business owners
- Highlighting early wins through local media as signals, not just stories
- Connecting experienced operators with new entrants
- Treating every successful business as a case study for replication

Because the goal is no longer inspiration. The goal is repeatability.

At the same time, entrepreneurs themselves must begin thinking beyond a single revenue stream. Rural markets reward those who understand how to layer income. This is where Hybrid Models become essential—not as a growth hack, but as a survival strategy that turns into strength.

A restaurant that also caters.
A retail shop that also sells online.
A service business that also teaches, hosts, or contracts.

These models do more than increase income. They stabilize it. They make the business more resilient to seasonality, population limits, and economic swings. And most importantly, they make the business more bankable.

Because consistent revenue is what capital recognizes.

Now the flywheel is beginning to accelerate.

The Midnight Moment sparked the first action

Deliberate Spending created visible circulation

The Main Street Entrepreneur turned that circulation into proof

And that proof is what unlocks the next phase:

Capital begins to move.

Not because it was invited—but because it can now see.

Local banks begin to take conversations more seriously.
Property owners begin to reconsider vacant buildings as assets.
Private individuals begin to see investment, not just risk.

The signal has changed.

The town is no longer a question mark. It is becoming a case.

And this is where the rural revolution either compounds—or stalls.

Because once capital starts to move, the most important question is no longer whether it comes, but who controls it.

That is the next phase of the system.

Because if ownership leaves, the flywheel breaks.
If ownership stays, the flywheel compounds.

And that is where we go next.

CHAPTER 9: THE NEW RURAL ECONOMY

The Leakage Plug

The Thesis:

A rural economy does not fail because it lacks money—it fails because it cannot keep it.

Wealth does not disappear all at once. It leaves in small, repeated decisions. A purchase made out of town. A service that does not exist locally. A supplier chosen by habit instead of proximity. Over time, these decisions compound until the town becomes a pass-through system—money comes in, but it does not stay.

This is not a demand problem. It is a retention problem.

The new rural economy shifts the focus. Not just attracting dollars, but holding them in motion long enough to matter. Story may attract attention, but circulation builds strength.

Protocol 9.1: The Leakage Audit

Identifying Where the Town Is Losing Every Week

Most towns try to build new businesses before understanding what they are already losing. They assume a lack of demand when, in reality, demand is simply being met somewhere else. Residents are already spending money—just not locally.

The work begins with a simple question: What are our residents leaving town to buy every single week? Not annually. Not hypothetically. Weekly. Food, repairs, healthcare, retail, essential services. These are not guesses; they are proven transactions.

Where money consistently leaves, opportunity already exists.

(Flywheel Tie-In: The Midnight Moment — Clear gaps reduce perceived risk and trigger action.)

Protocol 9.2: The Weekly Spend Map

Following the First 72 Hours

Once leaks are identified, the next step is to follow the flow. Where does a paycheck go within the first 24, 48, and 72 hours? This is where the real economy lives—not in projections, but in habits.

Most spending is predictable. And predictable spending builds stable businesses. This is the foundation of Main Street—not one large win, but thousands of repeated transactions.

(Flywheel Tie-In: Deliberate Spending — Awareness directs dollars with intention.)

Protocol 9.3: The Local Multiplier Effect

Turning Transactions into Momentum

Not all dollars behave the same. A locally spent dollar moves—it pays someone, who spends it again, who hires someone else. It circulates. A non-local dollar exits. Transaction complete. No second pass.

The difference is structural.

This is why spending is not just consumption—it is economic construction. Every dollar either strengthens the system or weakens it.

(Flywheel Tie-In: Retained Wealth — Circulation strengthens the lockbox.)

Protocol 9.4: The Leakage Plug

Capturing What Already Exists

Once a town sees its leaks clearly, it stops guessing and starts building with precision. The strongest rural businesses do not invent demand; they capture it. They step into categories where money is already leaving and reduce friction the community is already paying for.

This lowers risk. It increases survivability. And it creates businesses rooted in reality, not speculation.

(Flywheel Tie-In: Community Prosperity — Stability compounds through consistency.)

The Outcome: A Circulating Economy

When leakage is reduced, the system begins to shift. Money stays longer. Businesses stabilize. Confidence increases. One decision reinforces the next, and momentum builds—quietly at first, then visibly.

A town that once felt limited begins to feel capable. That is a Culture of Possibility. And it is built the same way the economy is built: one decision at a time.

CHAPTER 10: LOCAL OWNERSHIP

The Local Ownership Playbook

The Thesis:

- A town does not control its future unless it owns it.
- Activity is not ownership, and jobs are not control. A business can operate in a town and still have no long-term commitment to it. When ownership lives somewhere else, so do the decisions—and eventually, so does the future.
- A resilient economy is not built on one large employer. It is built on a diversified network of local owners.

Protocol 10.1: The Ownership Audit

Understanding Who Actually Controls the Economy

Many communities assume they are stable because businesses are open. But open does not mean owned. The Ownership Audit asks a harder question: who actually controls the assets?

- Who owns the buildings?
  Who owns the businesses?
  Where do the profits go?
  Who decides what happens next?
- A town can look active while being externally controlled. That is not stability. It is borrowed time.

(Flywheel Tie-In: Retained Wealth — Ownership determines what stays.)

Protocol 10.2: The Control Principle

Ownership Is Decision Power

Ownership determines outcomes. Stay or leave. Reinvest or extract. Expand or shut down. These are not local decisions if ownership is not local.

This is the real risk—not failure, but removal.

(Flywheel Tie-In: Community Prosperity — Stability requires control.)

Protocol 10.3: The Autonomy Layer

Protecting the Town from Outside Decisions

A town without ownership is exposed to forces it cannot control. Closures, consolidation, shifting priorities—these are structural decisions made elsewhere, but felt locally.

Autonomy means the town retains influence over what happens next. Not total independence, but enough control to protect what matters.

(Flywheel Tie-In: Deliberate Spending — Supporting local ownership reinforces control.)

Protocol 10.4: The Succession Handshake

Preserving What Has Already Been Built

The most fragile moment in a rural economy is not failure—it is transition. When a long-standing owner exits without a plan, the town faces a decision point: lose the business, sell it externally, or keep it local.

This is where Legacy Rescuers emerge. Not to start from zero, but to carry something forward. To preserve trust, continuity, and local control.

(Flywheel Tie-In: The Midnight Moment — Preservation becomes action.)

Protocol 10.5: Build-to-Stay Ownership

Strength Over Exit

Not all growth strengthens a town. Some growth extracts. Some growth removes control. The question becomes: does this deepen local ownership, or dilute it?

Healthy growth stays rooted. It expands without abandoning place. It builds something that can last.

(Flywheel Tie-In: Culture of Possibility — Ownership becomes attainable.)

The Outcome: Ownership with Authority

When ownership is local, everything changes. Decisions stay close. Profits stay longer. Responsibility becomes visible. Businesses think in decades, not quarters.

The town becomes more stable, more durable, and more confident—not because of one major employer, but because control is distributed across many hands.

That is what gives a community the ability to shape its own future.

CHAPTER 11: THE HOMECOMING PROTOCOL

Managing the Brain Gain

There is a lie many small towns tell themselves.

It sounds responsible.
It sounds realistic.
It even sounds mature.

It goes like this: our best people always have to leave.

For generations, rural communities have watched their most ambitious sons and daughters head toward cities, suburbs, and larger markets. They leave for college. They leave for work. They leave because they believe opportunity lives somewhere else.
In many cases, they are told that directly. If you want to build something, go somewhere bigger. If you want to make more money, go somewhere faster. If you want to matter, go where the action is.

And for a season, that often appears true.

Cities do concentrate opportunity. They offer scale, density, career ladders, investors, institutions, and professional networks. They expose people to systems, standards, and possibilities they may not have encountered back home. They sharpen skills. They build confidence. They generate income. They teach people how markets move, how brands are built, how organizations function, and how value is created.

But the rural mistake is assuming that departure is the end of the story.

It is not.

In a healthy local economy, departure can become part of the development pipeline. Some people leave not because they are rejecting home, but because they are gathering tools. They are accumulating experience, income, perspective, and competence. They are learning how larger systems work. They are building what we might call Urban Equity—skills, capital, networks, and pattern recognition acquired in more competitive environments.

Then one day, they look back.

They realize something the town itself often missed.

What looked small now looks open.
What looked limited now looks available.
What looked old now looks underpriced.
What looked ordinary now looks full of hidden leverage.

This is the beginning of the Homecoming Protocol.

The quiet revolution is not fueled only by people who never left. It is also fueled by people who left, learned, and came back ready to build. These returners are one of the most powerful forces in the rural economy because they combine outside capacity with inside loyalty. They understand the pace of larger markets, but they still care about a specific place. They know how to operate professionally, but they are not trying to extract and disappear. They bring back both competence and commitment.

That combination matters.

A town does not win merely by retaining every resident forever. A town wins when it creates conditions where people can return and convert what they learned elsewhere into local strength. This is not brain drain. This is brain gain. And if managed well, it becomes a major driver of the flywheel.

The Homecoming Protocol begins with a simple recognition: returning residents do not come back empty-handed. They come back with assets. Some of those assets are financial. Some are practical. Some are relational. Some are invisible at first glance. But they are real, and they can be turned into durable local advantage.

The first of these is quality of life arbitrage.

In a large metro, a talented person may spend years earning good money while bleeding away time, focus, and peace. Long commutes. Expensive housing. Endless traffic. Fragmented relationships. Constant overstimulation. High overhead touches everything. Even a strong income can feel thin when life is structured around stress. The result is a person who may be professionally successful but personally depleted.

A rural town can reverse that equation.

Shorter drives create time.
Lower housing costs create margin.
Familiar relationships create stability.
Less friction creates clarity.

These are not soft benefits. They are economic assets.

A person who gets back ten hours a week in commuting time has gained productive capacity. A family whose mortgage drops dramatically has gained financial flexibility. An entrepreneur who lives in a lower-cost market can operate with greater patience. A creative professional with more mental bandwidth can think better, serve better, and build better.

That is why quality of life is not a side perk in the rural economy. It is part of the business model. It creates what we can call Mental Capital—the restored energy, focus, and strategic patience that come from living in a lower-friction environment. In many cases, the returner is not stepping down economically. He is restructuring his life so that his talent works under less pressure and produces more durable results.

This matters to the first gear of the flywheel, The Midnight Moment. A return home often begins with a personal reckoning. A person decides he no longer wants to spend his life trapped inside a model that pays well but drains the soul. He decides to stop waiting for permission and start building where his life can actually fit together. That decision is not retreat. It is ignition.

The second part of the Homecoming Protocol is location-independent revenue.

This is where the modern rural economy changes the game.

In a previous era, leaving a major city often meant leaving major opportunity. But digital tools have broken that equation. Today, a consultant in a small town can serve clients in New York. A designer in a county seat can build brands for companies across the country.

A bookkeeper, strategist, media producer, software developer, coach, marketer, or agency owner can earn metropolitan revenue while living in a rural ZIP code.

That changes everything.

The old model required people to move to where the money was. The new model allows people to bring the money home.

This is one of the strongest strategies in the entire rural playbook. A returning entrepreneur who earns revenue from outside the region and spends, hires, gives, renovates, and invests locally becomes a force multiplier. He is effectively importing capital into the community. He is taking national dollars and routing them through local banks, local contractors, local coffee shops, local printers, local churches, local schools, and local nonprofits.

This directly strengthens Deliberate Spending, the second flywheel gear. Money earned elsewhere but spent locally turns the local multiplier faster. It plugs leakage. It increases circulation. It creates demand for other local businesses. A remotely earned dollar that lands on Main Street is often more powerful than a dollar that originated there, because it expands the pie instead of merely recirculating the existing slices.

And when that business is locally owned, it reinforces the third gear as well: Retained Wealth. The profit does not disappear into a distant headquarters. The decisions are not made in another state. The owner lives there. The family lives there. The property may be purchased there. The taxes are paid there. The children grow up there. The giving happens there. That is how local ownership converts individual success into community durability.

But there is another advantage returners bring, and it is often overlooked.

They come back with fresh eyes.

Longtime residents can miss the value of what is around them. Familiarity dulls perception. The old building becomes just the old building. The river becomes just the river. The downtown block becomes just the block you drive past every day. But someone who has lived elsewhere often sees differently. He has comparison points. He has seen what other places package, preserve, market, and monetize. He knows what outsiders pay for, what travelers notice, and what brands can be built around.

This is the Fresh Eye Audit.

What do we have that we have stopped seeing?
What local asset is hiding in plain sight?
What underused building could become a destination?
What overlooked story could become a brand?
What community habit could become an economic advantage?

A returner may notice that the town's old storefronts are not liabilities but atmosphere. He may realize that local food traditions are not ordinary but marketable. She may see that a neglected service gap is actually a viable business. He may understand that the lake, farm, timberland, architecture, festival, history, or downtown corridor has more value than locals assume. What insiders call normal, outsiders often call distinctive.

In North Florida, one example of this looks like a farm.

Jim—known through Field Rows—did not come back to start something new. He came back to what was already there: a working farm built on peanuts and cotton, operating on the same cycles it always had.

Like most farms, the model was simple. You plant, you wait, you harvest, and you get paid when the crop sells—once, maybe twice a year.

It worked, but it left long stretches where nothing was coming in.

None of that changed.

What changed was how he saw it.

"I started back in 2020... just doing YouTube," he said. It was nothing more than filming what was already happening.

Then something small broke through.

"I just had this old wig laying around..." he said. That became "Uncle

Randy."

That is what people responded to.

Not the polished version. The real one.

That was the shift.

The farm didn't change, but it stopped being just a production system. It became a platform.

For the first time, the operation had distribution.

And that changed the economics.

"With farming, you get paid when you sell your crop... maybe twice a year," Jim said.

Then he added something that doesn't usually belong in a farming conversation:

- "It's nice... making money while you're sleeping."
- That second stream didn't replace the farm.
- It stabilized it.
- "My day job is running a farm," he said.
- That never changed.
- What changed was that the farm could now carry more than crops.
- It could carry attention.
  It could carry revenue.
  It could carry reach.
- That is the difference between a farmer and an Ag-preneur.

The asset stays the same.

The output expands.

This is where Story as Economic Signal begins working again.

Returners are often translators. They can take the raw material of a place and frame it in language the market understands. They know how to position, package, communicate, and elevate what the town already has. In doing so, they strengthen the final gear of the flywheel: Culture of Possibility. Their return sends a signal. It tells the community that home is not a dead end. It tells young people that ambition and local loyalty do not have to be enemies. It tells the market that something is happening here.

That signal matters more than most towns realize.

When one capable person comes home and builds something visible, others start reconsidering their assumptions. A closed mental loop breaks open. The question changes from Why would anyone come back? to What would it look like if more did? That is how a culture shifts. Not through slogans, but through examples.

The Homecoming Protocol, then, is not about nostalgia. It is not a sentimental plea for people to move back just because they grew up there. Sentiment alone is not enough. The return has to make strategic sense. The town must offer enough openness, enough affordability, enough relational gravity, and enough room to build. The returner must be able to convert Urban Equity into local traction.

When that happens, the effect is profound.

The person returns with skills.
Returns with standards.
Returns with confidence.
Returns with capital.
Returns with perspective.
Returns with hunger.
And most importantly, returns with choice.

That last piece matters. Chosen homecoming is powerful. A person who comes back because he wants to build is very different from a person who feels trapped. One arrives with intention. And intention changes outcomes.

The future of many rural communities will not depend entirely on attracting strangers. It will depend on reactivating people who already carry the town in their bones. People who know the roads, know the names, know the rhythms, and know what has been lost. People who went away long enough to learn what works elsewhere, then came back ready to apply it with discipline and affection.

That is not backward movement.

That is strategic return.

And when enough of those returns begin to stack, a town starts to feel it.

A building gets renovated.
A storefront lights back up.
A service gap gets filled.
A national paycheck starts landing in a local bank.
A family commits.
A street gains momentum.
A younger generation notices.

This is how the quiet revolution advances.

Not always through expansion outward.

Sometimes through return inward.

And when managed well, brain gain becomes one of the strongest economic development strategies a rural town has.

CHAPTER 12: THE COMMUNITY OPERATING SYSTEM
Moving from "Town" to "Ecosystem"

A town does not become economically alive by accident.

It becomes alive when enough people begin acting as if growth is possible.

That is the real shift. Not from poor to rich. Not from old to new. Not even from struggling to thriving.

The shift is from passive place to active ecosystem.

This is where many communities get stuck. They may have good people, decent buildings, local history, and even a few determined business owners. But they still operate like a collection of isolated efforts instead of a connected local economy. One merchant is trying to survive. One banker is making cautious loans. One mayor is talking about revitalization. One chamber director is planning an event. One family is wondering whether to leave or stay. None of those actions are meaningless. But until they begin working in coordination, the town remains fragmented.

And fragmentation is expensive.

It makes every entrepreneur feel like they are building alone. It makes every vacant storefront feel more permanent than it really is. It makes every promising idea feel riskier than it should. A disconnected town drains momentum because nobody knows where support starts or who is supposed to carry the next piece of the load.

That is why entrepreneurship is a team sport.

The entrepreneur may be the visible builder, but the environment around that builder determines how far the effort can go. A community either lowers friction or adds to it. It either creates belief or spreads doubt. It either sends signals that say, "This is a place where things can happen," or it quietly trains people to expect decline.

That operating environment matters more than most towns realize.

Because what we are really talking about here is economic culture.

Every town has one.

Some towns celebrate builders. Others scrutinize them. Some towns tell stories of possibility. Others repeat stories of loss so often that decline starts to feel like identity. Some towns instinctively ask, "How can we help this work?" Others default to, "That will never work here."

Over time, those habits become a system.

And systems create outcomes.

If Chapter 11 was about the returning builder bringing back outside skills, capital, and perspective, then Chapter 12 is about whether the local environment knows what to do with that energy once it arrives. The returning entrepreneur may have the spark. But the town must have enough connective tissue to keep the engine running. This is where the flywheel either gains traction or stalls. This is where a Culture of Possibility stops being a slogan and starts becoming infrastructure.

A community operating system is simply this: the shared habits, signals, relationships, and civic decisions that make entrepreneurship easier to start, easier to support, and easier to sustain.

If you want a rural economy to grow, you cannot just cheer for entrepreneurs after they take the risk.

You have to build the kind of town that makes taking the risk feel reasonable.

That begins with narrative.

Every town is telling itself a story all the time. It happens in local media, in Facebook comments, at the coffee shop, in church parking lots, in city meetings, and at Friday night ballgames. The question is not whether the town has a narrative. The question is whether that narrative is producing movement or paralysis.

In too many places, the dominant script is still decline.

We used to be bigger. We used to have more jobs. We used to have more stores. Young people do not stay. Nothing ever lasts. Nobody supports local. Every building that closes becomes further proof that the script is true.

That script is deadly.

Not because hardship is imaginary, but because repeated language shapes what people are willing to attempt. When decline becomes the default story, caution starts masquerading as wisdom. Skepticism starts masquerading as experience. Eventually the town becomes emotionally organized around disappointment, and new builders must fight not only market conditions but the expectations of the people around them.

That is too much drag on the system.

A healthy community operating system intentionally replaces the decline script with possibility stories.

Not fantasy. Not hype. Not fake boosterism.

Proof.

Proof that someone renovated a building. Proof that a family came back. Proof that a small shop expanded. Proof that an old property found new life. Proof that a local service business is quietly making payroll and building something durable. Proof that the town is still capable of producing builders.

That is why local storytelling matters so much. Media is not just information. It is signal. It tells residents what matters, what is possible, and what kind of future deserves attention. When local media, local leaders, and everyday conversation begin highlighting builders instead of only problems, they start changing the emotional weather of the town. And emotional weather matters in economic development more than most spreadsheets can measure.

A community cannot grow if it only knows how to memorialize what it lost.

It has to learn how to publicize what is being built.

That narrative work connects directly to the flywheel. It strengthens the Midnight Moment by giving potential entrepreneurs visible evidence that action is possible. It feeds Deliberate Spending by reminding residents that local businesses are not abstractions but neighbors worth backing. It reinforces Retained Wealth by making local ownership something the community recognizes as valuable. And it contributes to Community Prosperity by helping people imagine a different future together. Most of all, it builds the Culture of Possibility that allows the whole system to keep turning.

But story alone is not enough.

Belief must be matched with support.

That is where connective tissue comes in.

Most small towns do not fail because nobody cares. They fail because the caring is uncoordinated. The chamber is doing one thing. The bank is doing another. Experienced business owners have useful wisdom but no pathway to share it. City officials want growth but are buried in process. New entrepreneurs do not know who to call, where to start, or how to avoid basic mistakes.

So they end up isolated.

Isolation is one of the most under-discussed forms of economic friction in rural communities. The entrepreneur feels like the only one taking risk. The family opening a storefront does not know whether financing is realistic. The person with an idea for a service business has no mentor. The returner with skills from outside the market has no obvious entry point into local relationships. Good people with viable ideas lose momentum not because the idea is bad, but because the path is lonely and confusing.

A town with a healthy operating system reduces that isolation.

It creates a visible support network.

That does not require a massive bureaucracy. In fact, it usually works better when it stays simple. A community needs local bankers willing to explain options instead of just saying no. It needs seasoned business owners willing to share hard-earned lessons. It needs civic leaders who understand that small businesses are not interruptions to public life but part of the town's future. It needs chambers and development groups that act less like event planners and more like connectors. It needs informal introductions, practical checklists, warm handoffs, and real relationships.

The goal is not to remove risk.

The goal is to remove unnecessary confusion.

A builder should still have to work. They should still have to prove demand, manage cash flow, and survive the normal hardships of business ownership. But they should not have to waste half their strength figuring out who handles signage, whether a lender might be open to the conversation, which contractor to trust, or whether anybody in town wants them to succeed.

That is what connective tissue does. It shortens the distance between ambition and action.

And then there is the civic layer.

This is where many communities misunderstand economic development. They think growth begins when outside investors suddenly discover them. But private investment rarely moves first without signals. It follows confidence. It follows visible order. It follows cues that say this place is serious about itself.

That is where local government and civic leadership matter.

Not because they can manufacture prosperity on their own, but because they can create conditions that invite it.

Zoning matters. Sign ordinances matter. Sidewalks matter. Lighting matters. Code enforcement matters. Storefront presentation matters. Landscaping matters. Parking matters. Clean public spaces matter. None of these things are cosmetic in the deeper sense. They are economic signals. They tell residents, visitors, investors, and entrepreneurs whether the town expects stagnation or is preparing for activity.

Blight communicates surrender.

Order communicates readiness.

A cracked sidewalk, a dark block, a confusing approval process, or a neglected downtown may seem like minor issues when discussed one at a time. But together they create a message. They tell builders that they will be fighting uphill. They tell lenders that momentum is weak. They tell families considering a move that this may not be a place worth betting on.

The opposite is also true.

A clean corridor, thoughtful beautification, walkable pockets, preserved historic character, and reasonable processes send a very different message. They say: people here are paying attention. They say: investment will be noticed and reinforced. They say: this town is not waiting to die.

That is civic buy-in.

Not endless committees. Not vanity projects. Not generic "revitalization" language.

Real alignment between public stewardship and private courage.

When that alignment begins to happen, a town stops behaving like a loose collection of buildings and starts behaving like an ecosystem. One improvement supports another. One win becomes cover for the next risk. One returning entrepreneur changes how another person sees the town. One beautified block makes one more lease feel possible. One possibility story gives one more family the courage to stay, return, buy, launch, or reinvest.

That is how ecosystems form.

Slowly at first.

Then all at once.

The town begins to understand that economic culture is not abstract. It is built decision by decision, story by story, handshake by handshake, storefront by storefront. It is carried in what people celebrate, what they tolerate, what they repair, what they permit, what they encourage, and what they expect.

A rural economy becomes durable when entrepreneurship is no longer treated like a lonely exception.

It becomes part of the local operating system.

And once that happens, the town is no longer just a place on a map.

It becomes a living network of belief, support, and coordinated action.

It becomes an ecosystem.

And ecosystems know how to grow.

CHAPTER 13: THE MANIFESTO

The Quiet Revolution Mandate

Every book like this must end with a line in the sand.

Not a soft conclusion.
Not a polite summary.
A mandate.

Because by now the pattern should be clear. The future of the American economy will not be secured by a handful of superstar cities alone. It will not be built only in glass towers, venture-backed corridors, or zip codes already overflowing with capital. It will be built in the places too many experts wrote off. It will be built in county-seat towns, farm communities, fishing towns, crossroads communities, and old railroad places that still have more strength in them than the national narrative knows how to measure.

The American economy is decentralizing.

Not all at once.
Not neatly.
But undeniably.

Technology has untethered opportunity from geography. Talent is more mobile. Work is more flexible. Customers can be reached from anywhere. Knowledge that once pooled only in major metros now travels instantly. A founder in a rural county can serve a client in Dallas, Nashville, or

New York without leaving town. A small business can build a national audience from a Main Street storefront. A returning son or daughter can bring back skills, capital, and perspective that once would have been trapped elsewhere.

That changes everything.

It means the old assumption—that ambition must leave home to matter—is breaking apart. It means the economic map of America is being redrawn in real time. And it means the places prepared to recognize this shift will have an opportunity to build something durable, rooted, and deeply human.

That is the mandate of the quiet revolution.

This book has argued one central idea from the beginning: rural prosperity does not begin with rescue from the outside. It begins when local people decide to build with what they have, where they are, for the long haul. It begins when a town stops seeing itself as a leftover place and starts seeing itself as a place of strategic advantage. It begins when builders, business owners, local institutions, and civic leaders all begin acting as if the future is still available to them.

Because it is.

That is the first thing this manifesto demands: reject the decline script.

The decline script is seductive because it sounds wise. It sounds informed. It sounds realistic. It says the best days are gone. It says all the talent leaves. It says small towns cannot compete. It says ownership will consolidate, local identity will fade, and the only reasonable response is nostalgia mixed with managed retreat.

But the decline script is not wisdom.

It is surrender disguised as analysis.

Yes, many places have lost population. Yes, some downtowns have emptied out. Yes, local institutions have weakened. Yes, wealth has leaked, ownership has consolidated, and too many communities have been taught to think of themselves as dependent rather than generative. All of that is real. But decline is not destiny. It is a condition.

And conditions can be changed.

That is what entrepreneurism does.

It interrupts drift.
It restores motion.
It turns possibility into structure.

Every local business that fills a service gap does more than make a profit. It reduces friction in daily life. Every renovated storefront sends a signal that someone believes the future is worth investing in. Every locally-owned company that chooses durability over extraction helps keep wealth circulating longer inside the community (Deliberate Spending). Every founder who decides to stay and build helps anchor ownership where it matters most (Retained Wealth). Every successful enterprise that hires, serves, and endures adds visible proof that the town is not finished (Community Prosperity). And every story told about that progress helps create the narrative climate in which the next builder believes they can act too (Culture of Possibility).

That is the flywheel.

Not theory.
Not branding.
A working civic mechanism.

And once you see it, you cannot unsee it.

A town is not merely a collection of buildings and roads. It is an operating system of beliefs, signals, incentives, habits, and relationships. If that operating system rewards caution, mocks risk, and romanticizes only the past, it will produce stagnation. If it celebrates problem-solvers, supports small ownership, and treats every act of local building as meaningful, it will produce motion.

That is why the revolution is quiet.

Because it rarely arrives as spectacle.
It arrives as stewardship.

A couple buys the old business instead of letting it close. A local founder opens the service everyone has been driving thirty miles to get. A lender says yes to a borrower they know will stand behind the work. A chamber starts highlighting renovations instead of funerals. A newspaper runs possibility stories instead of recycling despair. A returning family brings home outside income and reinvests it locally. A business owner decides not to chase scale for vanity's sake, but to build something that can still be standing in twenty years.

None of that looks flashy in the moment.

But that is how places change.

This manifesto also demands a redefinition of success.

For too long, Americans have been trained to think that success means bigger, faster, farther, more. More units. More square footage. More exits. More scale. More abstraction. More distance between the builder and the place being affected.

But that model, left unchecked, creates fragility. It often extracts more than it roots. It rewards growth without always asking what kind of growth is being created, who owns it, or whether the gains remain in the place that generated them.

Rural entrepreneurism offers a different scorecard.

Stewardship over scale.

That does not mean small for the sake of small. It does not mean weak ambition. It does not mean refusing growth. It means growth is judged by whether it strengthens the place, not merely the balance sheet. It means durability matters more than bragging rights. It means local ownership matters because ownership determines who decides, who benefits, and who stays when conditions get hard. It means building enterprises that are rooted enough to endure and flexible enough to adapt.

The goal is not to be the biggest.

The goal is to be the most durable.

A durable business can train employees, support families, weather hard seasons, reinvest locally, and become part of the civic memory of a place. A durable business can outlast trends. It can become an institution. It can create continuity where instability once ruled. In a rural town, that kind of business does not simply participate in the economy. It helps hold the economy together.

That is the assignment.

Build ventures that stay.
Build ventures that circulate money.
Build ventures that keep ownership close.
Build ventures that make the next builder's risk a little lower.

And beyond business, this chapter issues one final challenge to civic leaders, publishers, pastors, bankers, property owners, mentors, and long-time residents.

You are not spectators in this process.

You are either increasing friction or reducing it.

You are either sending signals of possibility or signals of decay. You are either helping builders navigate the terrain or forcing them to fight isolation alone. You are either treating local entrepreneurism as a side story or recognizing it as the central work of community renewal.

Places do not become resilient by accident.
They become resilient when enough people decide to act like resilience is their responsibility.

Which brings us to the final audit.

Every project must answer one question:

Will this place be stronger because this business existed?

That question cuts through vanity.
It cuts through trend-chasing.
It cuts through hollow growth.

It forces the founder, the investor, the lender, the landlord, and the local leader to tell the truth. Did this enterprise leave behind stronger habits, stronger ownership, stronger trust, stronger skills, stronger circulation, stronger belief? Did it deepen the roots of the place, or merely use the place as a platform?

That is the standard.

Because the quiet revolution is not about romanticizing rural America. It is about rebuilding it. It is not about preserving towns as museum pieces. It is about making them economically alive again. It is not about waiting for permission from national gatekeepers. It is about local people recovering the confidence to build systems of prosperity with their own hands.

The future will belong to places that understand this.

Places that learn to keep talent connected.
Places that reward courage.
Places that keep money moving locally.
Places that protect ownership.
Places that tell better stories.
Places that choose stewardship over spectacle.
Places that stop apologizing for their size and start leveraging their strengths.

The revolution will not always be loud.

But it will be visible.

It will be visible in lit storefronts and occupied buildings. In businesses passed down instead of boarded up. In young families returning home with something to build. In local brands with national reach. In a downtown that feels claimed again. In a community that no longer talks like a victim of history, but like a participant in the future.

That is the mandate.

Build where you are.
Keep what you can.
Back the people who stay.
Tell better stories.
Choose durability.
Create proof.
Spin the flywheel.

Quietly, if you must. But start now.

FIELD NOTES

Mark what matters. Record what happens. Run it again.

Date: ____________ Location: ____________ Protocol: ____________

PINE CONE PRESS

AFTER YOU RUN THE FIRST PROTOCOL

Do not wait for the whole town to agree.

Find one visible gap.
Name one useful action.
Bring in one serious person.
Run one protocol.

Then watch what moves.

The work does not begin when the plan is perfect.
It begins when someone takes responsibility for motion.

Run the first protocol.
Record what happened.
Then run the next one.

**THE RURAL REVOLUTION IS NOT A MOMENT.
IT IS A SYSTEM IN MOTION.**

theruralrevolution.com

· PINE CONE PRESS ·

www.ingramcontent.com/pod-product-compliance
Lightning Source LLC
LaVergne TN
LVHW010738061126
851857LV00014B/1543